by Tom Clark

Airplanes (1966)
The Sandburg (1966)
Emperor of the Animals (1967)
Bun (1968)
Stones (1969)
Air (1970)
Car Wash (1970)
Neil Young (1971)
The No Book (1971)
Green (1971)
Smack (1972)
John's Heart (1972)
Back in Boston (1972)
Blue (1974)
Chicago (1974)
Suite (1974)
At Malibu (1975)
Fan Poems (1976)
Baseball (1976)
Champagne and Baloney (1976)
35 (1976)
No Big Deal (1977)
How I Broke In (1977)
The Mutabilitie of the Englishe Lyrick (1978)
When Things Get Tough on Easy Street: Selected Poems
     1963–1978 (1978)
The World of Damon Runyon (1978)
One Last Round for The Shuffler (1979)
The Master (1979)
Who Is Sylvia? (1979)
The Great Naropa Poetry Wars (1980)
The Last Gas Station and Other Stories (1980)
The End of the Line (1980)
A Short Guide to the High Plains (1981)
Heartbreak Hotel (1981)
The Rodent Who Came To Dinner (1981)
Journey to the Ulterior (1981)
Nine Songs (1981)
Under the Fortune Palms (1982)
Dark As Day (1983)
Writer: A Life of Jack Kerouac (1984)
Paradise Resisted: Selected Poems 1978–1984 (1984)
Property (1984)
The Border (1985)
Late Returns: A Memoir of Ted Berrigan (1985)
His Supposition (1986)
Kerouac's Last Word (1986)
The Exile of Céline (1987)
Disordered Ideas (1987)

TOM CLARK

DISORDERED

IDEAS

BLACK
SPARROW
PRESS
SANTA
ROSA
1987

ACKNOWLEDGEMENTS

Some of the poems in this book first appeared in the following publications: *The Baltimore Sun, Berkeley Works, City Lights Review, Clock Radio, Emigré, Equator, Exquisite Corpse, Infolio, Poetry Flash, The Poetry Project Newsletter, Processed World, Rolling Stock, Shiny Magazine, This Is Important, Volition, Writers Outside the Margin, The Worm in the Rain,* and *Zyzzyva.*

"The Eleven O'Clock News" appeared as a Bloody Twin Press broadside.

LIBRARY OF CONGRESS CATALOGING-IN-PUBLICATION DATA
Clark, Tom, 1941–
  Disordered ideas.

  I. Title.
PS3553.L29D5   1987   811'.54   87-5211
ISBN 0-87685-696-2
ISBN 0-87685-697-0 (signed)
ISBN 0-87685-695-4 (pbk.)

Table of Contents

A Citizen of the Future

Disordered Ideas

DISORDERED IDEAS

"To write poetry now, even on current events, means to withdraw into the ivory tower. It's as though one were practicing the art of filigree. There is something eccentric, cranky, obtuse about it. Such poetry is like the castaway's note in the bottle."

—Bertolt Brecht, 1942

The Dollmaker (Hans Bellmer)

Bellmer tied up Unica Zurn
with string
creating
new shapes out of her body
and then photographed her
later she leapt
100 feet to her death

In 1924
he created his Doll
whose ball-jointed pelvis
made possible
amazing displacements
of its parts

Then we see
Bellmer in the basement
of the rue Mouffetard
called by his neighbors
"the man in black"
not for his noir vision
but for the color
of his turtleneck

We look down at his hand
that right hand
which created his Doll
the hand which someone
a woman
once described
as not the hand of the artist
or a lover

but a murderer's hand
it's with a life of its own
that the hand rises
and moves across the basement room
to the drafting board

Why does Bellmer's
art express so well
the fallenness of men
their existence under this Spell
as if out of each one
had come another
who walks beside him
and bears his name
but feels nothing

Saying this I hear
a hellish laughter
starting up
in heaven
and then a voice that asks
could it be
we did not fall
but were pushed
like Bellmer's dolls
as they dropped from
the Dollmaker's arms

Sadly Céline

Sadly Céline
in death was spoken
of not so much
for the work which
brought with it
such inconsistencies
of character, as
for the latter. A

text is variously
a life, but the purpose
of an individual
is single.
To be difficult
is to be difficult.
There are no two
ways about it.

Céline Again

The world not
the abuser, the
poor single
thing inside
the person's skin
not the
abused. And
yet, and
yet.

Wrong from the Start

The path of least resistance
is a straight line
but once you deviate
even slightly
the path of least
resistance becomes
that of greater
and greater
deviation

'Fault'

Turns out
from the beginning
what's 'wrong'
with some person
is largely 'fault'
of chromosomes
which won't ever
take the 'blame'
in the end

Double

in cell division
two threads
like split ends
hairs splitting
streaming into the trees
of gene forest
in background
of tapestry
in foreground
clotho
spinner of fates
asleep at wheel
drops one stitch
in spiral helix
genes shake loose
connective tissue
un-knits
its miracles
soul unravels
every time
mitosis occurs
in cell division
two threads

Vanity of Duluoz

"People have changed so much
No more sincere guys handsapocket walking"

Kerouac came back to Lowell with Johnny Walker
On his back like

A nasty monkey. Saying: "Mother
Nature gives you birth and eats you back up,

That's the ballgame . . ."

This was not a theory.
This was his cells talking.

Miles Davis

squeaks through
vocal chords
sandpapered
by all that blowing

what can I say
about the instrument
it's my voice

The Shield of Charles Olson

The shield of Charles Olson
is his pedagogic address

This large hand
held discourse
upon which
the incoming storm of
accidentals
makes only a few
cosmetic dents

Holds students at arms
length
while letting in cosmos
to the Max

Bed at Tor House

Jeffers when he built the house chose
the bed downstairs by the sea window
for his death bed. For years it went
unused except by occasional guests
who of course never suspected what
the designer of the house had in mind
for it. Jeffers kept his purpose
as he kept most of life's unsayableness
pretty much to himself. Not that
the bed wasn't of interest to him.
Walking through the room he often glanced
at it with the calm neutral attention
of a man looking into a piece of crystal.
Years flaked away. He waited by the sea
safe to finish what he had to finish
and looking forward without particular
distress to the day when the old
guy who'd produced this movie of
sky   sea   rock   in the first
place would thump his staff
and in a voice silted with
gravel salt and sand of the place
call "Come, Jeffers" three times.

Caspar David Friedrich and the Interior Dictation of Landscape

He avoided Goethe's invitations to come to Weimar
and work together on a collaboration
He was too busy collaborating with certain beings
inside him
whose commands he found so much more compelling
they came alive
during his solitary strolls into the countryside at dawn
or just after moonrise
his favorite time
during which he often paused to sketch
a group of trees a cloud a boulder a row of dunes or a tuft of grass
at their urging
Every true work of art he wrote *is conceived in a sacred hour*
and born
from an inner impulse of the heart

As he grew older depression distanced him more
and more
from the world of men
I have to be
on my own
and I have to know I am on my own
so that I can give myself up to what is around me
he wrote
in declining an invitation to tour the Alps
with a Russian poet
who admired his paintings
I have to unite with my clouds and rocks
I have to unite with everything around me
in order to be what I am

When the mineral world dissolves into the cosmic flux
the animal and vegetable worlds will have been long gone
but the beings who existed inside Friedrich and dictated his
        landscapes
will still be carving vast silences out of elemental gulfs

He had a special interest in the moon
He used to say
that if after death men were transported to another place
then he would prefer one less terrestrial than lunar
in order to allow the beings inside him to feel at home

Friedrich's Dream

Caspar David Friedrich's
technique of gathering
empty pastures of light
saturated with a kind
of tragic radiation
on the middle of his canvases
came to him in a dream

When he worked
at painting a sky
no one was permitted
to enter his studio
because he believed
God was present

Friedrich's Vision

When Friedrich walks
beside the shimmering
melancholy Baltic

what he sees with his eyes
is sandy dunes and reeds
and tufts of bunch-grass

but what he sees in his mind
is great blank skies
through which at intervals

tall clouds move
in vast parabolas
over gloomy summits

whose lower zones
are enclosed in mists and fogs
and a crepuscular kind of light

that lets ancient fir trees
hoist their vaults
in quiet contemplation

of the eternity
in one patch of moss
on the side of a rock

Friedrich's Vision (II)

In the distance the blue mountains melt away into sky
Swirling mists of the river swallow up the small boat
A slight almond green sheen blankets and glazes
The canvas with a sense of vast mass and the
Imminent accession of a sky-exploding eternity.

Friedrich's Rejoinder

Caspar David Friedrich strolled with Brahms and Novalis
late one night along the Baltic
among ghostly moors from which thin reeds poked up.
"Everything here has a soul in tune with my own," Brahms said.
"A magic spell towers above the restless water," Novalis answered.
"When one is under the influence of choloroform,"
Caspar David Friedrich said, "one must not speak of such things."

Rimbaud

Despairing
of finding a way out
of industrial society
Jean-Arthur
Rimbaud
invented
the future
to do his
work for him
and then resigned
He knew
poetry
isn't worth dying
for
That left everything
else

Like an actor
much too youthful
of face
for the role
of Macbeth
he had to grow
into the part
written for him
when
he went
to Africa
to play out
the mercantile
gesture
of his class

The theory
that
the attitude
of the footloose
vagabond
who puts
himself at
the mercy
of chance
and turns
his back
on society
paves the way
for later
less risky
investments
is proven
by what happened
to him there

In the last
spasm of 19c.
capitalism
bourgeois
adventurers
from all over
Europe
were steaming off
to exotic
continents
Mexico
Somaliland
the Crimea
chasing a wave
of profit
whose true dividends
Rimbaud

himself had
first sighted
in The
Drunken
Boat
a poem that
first imitated
and then
terminated
for all time
the colonial
pastoral
idyll
by making it describe
not the Escape
of some eccentric
bohemian
poet
lolling
in the country
in velvet jeans
but that
of a man
no longer
able
to exist
inside the
sociology
of his class

What did Rimbaud
seek
in that Africa
of black trees
and dust

Gold

Not the philosopher's
stone
but the real thing
Did he find
it
No
What did he find
Exporting
of hides
coffee
musk
various business
in guns
in which he found
himself
being cheated
by Menelik
King of Choa
etc. not
to mention
a small
piece of the action
in slave
traffic

In the end
the spent crest
of the wave
deposited him
where history
always does
death
a dialectical
beginning
perhaps but
in this case
of what

What did Rimbaud
believe in
Nothing
What did he leave
behind
One leg
his memory
art
the 20c.
the language
of colors
poetry
flies
gulfs of darkness
the greenish
down
on the inside
of blond
gods' thighs
the lines
"Bathed
in your
languor
O wave
I care
no more
to sail
in the wake
of the cotton
boats
or undergo
the pride of flags"

Rimbaud and the Death of Poetry

Rimbaud said:
"Heaven is
what escaped
from the poem"

Poetry's a product
of becoming
There's nothing wrong
with the Hegelian
notion of it
withering away
along with the rest of art
into mere employment
for the idle
dinner music
and the fetishism
of the commodity
our liking
or not liking these facts
won't alter them
Reality only listens
when your words
are true
Rimbaud's Rx
for the poem
114 years ago
"one
must be absolutely
new"
was the expression of
an unconscious
hunch

both stating
his disgust
with the stale
and the familiar
and intuitively
anticipating
the history
of modern art
much as
his later
incommunicado stance
on becoming
a co-opted
employee
anticipated
its decline

In the end
time
will put a stop
to the use
of the poem
as fetish
and what will
remain
will be proof
of Rimbaud's dictum
that poetry
should not say
what has never been
nor what may yet come
but must always wish
for it to come about
"the poet"
he announced
"by long
and well-thought-
out

disordering
of all the senses
must make himself
a criminal
in order to arrive
at the Unknown"

In 1880
he finds work
as a buyer
with Bardey
& Co.
dealer
in coffee & hides
five
years later
he informs Bardey
he's "once known
poets
and artists
and so on
in the Latin Quarter"
but has
"seen enough
of those birds
to last him at least
forever"
To poetry he offers only
silence after that
no more words
a priest
who has turned his back
on his own altar

1880

"O god I am lost
in the intoxicating
fetish
of the Kunstwerk"

That is the delusion
of the youthful
speaking
The artist in his velvet
jacket and beret
who proceeds
painfully
and by many slow
but necessary changes
to the much belated
realization
that
the gloves of construction
were too heavy
for him to lift
in the first place
much less
the foundation
beams
of a work
someone could live
and move around in

Africa — 1891

"What a pain in the ass
this life is!"

That sentence
more succinct
in meaning
than anything else in
his final telegram
from Aden
That was poetry's gift
from the exhausted
Rimbaud
a diffident
postscript
to his scornful
abandonment
of it
18 years earlier
when he'd kissed off
the Word
as if to shed
thereby
the death
penalty
of being
human

He'd once imagined
himself
addressing a firing
squad
"I've never

belonged
to this race
I don't grasp
its codes
I have no
moral sense
I'm an animal
you're
making
a bad
mistake"

Yet
if you see
Rimbaud's
life
as a poem
about the history
of the race
one
whose images
express
a repressed trek
to the Interior
in which everything goes
wrong
from the start
bugs
bad weather
diseases
negative
conjunctions of the stars
Space and Time
expand

Rimbaud stretched
the poem
the way Boeing

stretches a 727
to make it carry more
truth
payload
"I have tried"
he said later
"to invent
new flowers
new stars
new flesh
new tongues
I believed
I had acquired
supernatural
powers"
all that stretching
took a shoehorn
larger than
the Horn of Africa
making it all the
more dramatic
when
he later
folded it in
on itself
again
like a squashed accordion
admitting
he had been
"stuffed
with
lies"

Poetry in Alexandria

He brushed his thumb across
the strings exactly
as he'd been trained

That first strum
always brought back
the day he'd auditioned
for his Library
Appointment
shivering over
the story of Jason
despite the heat
in the poets' atrium

Once upon a time
positions for singers
had more or less
grown on trees
but under the current
Ptolemies
whose endless
dynastic wars
were like rusty spears
poking slow leaks
in the Library Budget
it was simpler for a man
to scale the Great Pyramid
with rocks tied to both feet
than to get a tenure track
appointment for poetry
at the Mouseion

Born far from here
across the
sea on an island
Exile reminded him
of standing
still
amid reeds
and looking down
the throat
of a crocodile
there was constantly
a sensation
of large bellows closing
below and above
and also
a nervous phantom
propinquity
to the click of huge teeth

One night
he stood
and watched
the beam
of the great
lighthouse
sweep out
over
the harbor
the Mediterranean
with its small
waves stretched
out to the
west
more numerous
than the myriad
manuscript scrolls
in the
Mouseion

he stroked
the strings
and sang
lines
that evoked
the strange
deep song
in the throat
of a nightingale
floating
unseen in
some dark
pocket of trees
a thousand miles
from here

Glancing now
over the heads of his listeners
into the fire
that guttered in the rocks
beyond
he gathered
his skills and began
to play

As his voice rose
the blackness of the
Egyptian night
color of Greek
olives
became alight
with the wild
phosphorescences of
red   blue and green
you sometimes see
over the ocean
in an electrical storm

"Come now Erato
stand by my side and
say next how Jason
brought back the fleece to
Iolcus aided by the
memory of the odor
inside Medea's shift
on a summer's morning
after she's showered—"
thinking of his own wife
left behind
two decades earlier
on a Greek island

His voice
swam on
across the night
till heads
swayed with it

"—and all the bitterness
of Phoebus
was assuaged"

Then he stayed
his lyre
and divine voice
but though he had ceased
his hushed listeners
still bent forward with eagerness
ears intent
on the charm of song
he had left behind in their hearts
so clearly
a strain
from Elsewhere
that for once
no one in the crowd

had the nerve to smile
and say behind his hand
"get a job!"

FIVE POEMS AFTER BRECHT

1. City Life

When I talk to you in a cold
impersonal tone
carefully selecting words
as hard
as kryptonite
and not looking at you
(as if I didn't know you
or even that you were there)
I'm only
talking to you
in reality's voice
(cold and dry
and bored
to death with you)
a fact which in my opinion
you're unable
to grasp

2. Black Saturday

In the spring borne aloft on green skies
And rough trade winds, the kind that always buoy me,
I dropped down into black cities,
My soul's insides papered with chilly statements yet to be
      uttered.

I exposed myself to dogs on black streets
I pumped black water into myself, heard black screams of lost
      souls
But all that, reader, still left me cold
and empty, giddy and lightheaded as before.

They knocked holes out through my walls
These things I kept inside me, they poured out
Proving there was nothing inside me but space
And silence—all I was was paper, so they swore.

I kept on falling, smiling, falling—between homes
Of men, out through drains into open country. Winds
Jet-streamed through my walls, now they had it easy
And in came the rain, and in came the snow.

Finally every barfly for miles could inform you
Without lifting snout from trough: there's nothing to me
But this voidzone mudpigs roll around in, down upon
Which birds drip slime from a milky sky.

Less substance in me than in that lowering sky!
Less than in the wind that slices through! I traveled on
Wings of my own poetry following a stork
Much swifter than myself, eastward toward dawn.

3. *The Opium Smoker*

You know a girl who every night loses herself in the black
        smoke
Is doomed to become a bride of nothingness
Can't be lowered later, also can't be uplifted
Two mornings out of three doesn't even seem to be alive.

Forgets about keeping her chin up, has no need to
Too late for that, her hair and looks are shot
Passing a shopwindow, sees reflected
Her new forgetful self: wonders who's that person.

Feels the smoke slip into her bloodstream, feels its fog slip
Soft fingers through her mind: sleeps solo to be near the soil
That's reeling her in so swiftly on an invisible thread.

Her existence is no longer known to her, only others
Whatever won't be noticed, she'll do promptly
Anything to keep in good with a girl's best friend.

4. Bad Teeth

What damage too much blackberry sugar left undone to them
Chopping them against each other in anger did
One must be innocent as a babe to accept the chastity of old age
In the middle of life: what's left is spent without profit.

Sure, my jaw is capable of crushing small stones
All by itself, as witness my gums' slate blue color
Don't get the impression it's because I'm vain about this
That I expose them by chewing like a performer.

Once upon a time I didn't have ten dollars
To my name, but I had several women
Who ever since my teeth started to rot away
No longer want to give me themselves or dinner.

The days when a mouthful of good enamel
Still flashed in my head unappreciated by them
Stand out all the clearer in my memory now as
The girls who loved me then slowly forget what I look like.

Steamed up about this at first, I cooled off
Later and turned instead to metaphysics
Which taught me being-in-itself and being-
For-others are differentiable only via alcohol.

5. Mortality

"Go ahead!" (That's what the doctor said) "Let your cigar
Go on imitating a chimney—whether you do or you don't
Sooner or later you're going to blow away
Like another lost wisp of industrial smoke!"

In the membrane of my eye there are already small lesions
The early stages of a cancer that'll do me in one day
But there's no reason as yet for me to panic
The disease could take half a decade to do its dirty work.

A man can go along for years, fattening himself up
On fried chicken and blackberries: meanwhile he knows
Consumption's bound to catch up with him in the long run
He can't expect to be rescued, whether by booze or by his
        business sense.

A cancer like this one will sneak up and jump you
In the end: until then it quietly bides its time
Who knows, maybe it'll pick the moment you ascend
The altar steps, bride on your arm, to start metastasizing.

Take my uncle for instance, who kept his pants pressed
Perfectly even though he'd soon be wearing them in a box
"His face still has a lot of color," people lied, "like flowers"
Yes, the kind they throw on after the last shovelful of dirt.

With some families cancer's the sap that drives the family
        tree
Not that they'd care to discuss that fact
They have no trouble distinguishing an herb from a pineapple
But telling a tumor from a hernia takes more courage than
        they've got.

My grandfather wasn't that type, he knew what was coming
Did everything the doctors told him to do
Made it all the way to fifty before the effort overcame him.
To live through one such day's a curse unfit for a dog.

You and I: we understand each other, don't we
Envy's pointless, each man faces his particular downfall
My own latest zone of decline seems to be the kidneys
They haven't allowed me to take a drink for over a year now.

Uses of Being

careermanagementwise
a writer can make few moves
more useful than justifying

submission to repression
the more somber and "profound"
the justification the better

when for example heidegger disguised
his own voice
as the voice of being

and with oracular gravity proclaimed
the historical situation of his time
ontologically legitimate

while hinting in quavering undertone
the perdido state of his dasein
a plea meant to be heard by eternity

eternity heard him
and handed him the keys
to the wine and cheese

not to mention the presidency
of the university
of freiburg

Despite its having acted for so long
as if it were the other way around

Philosophy owes the world a favor
all these years of claiming
to have the truth
up its sleeve
the clever deception
of a sleight of hand artist
after too many nights on the road
in front of disappointing houses
thousands of years
making words
vanish into the thin air
of concepts
leaves Philosophy a little ragged
around the edges
every time it pulls a fast one
some guy in the back row notices
and lets out a belly laugh
it needs two weeks in Florida
but will settle for a week in Vegas
or the Catskills

Vacuum

Mere thought
cannot stick substance
like a kind
of ontic Post-it
onto its theses
to make them literal

It can only talk
about things
in words
that when it's through with them
blow away
and drift
joining the floating mass
of space junk
that tumbles in orbit
around
the papier maché
planet

Bitter Pursuit

When Pascal's sister said, Blaise
just studies ways
to be pissed on
by the rest of the human race
she was missing
the sense in which one
who anticipates
the impossibility of slaking
his thirst for spirit
without also taking in
a mouthful of acid
comes at last to express
the whole truth
about a universe
reduced to
a single sour grape

Rilke

Rainer
Maria
with a woman's
name
and
habits
of accepting
compliments
from the beyond

the pet
poet
in the castle
kept
in groceries
by blue
haired ladies

he pricked
his finger
on a myth
and died
of it

in keeping with
the universal
theory
of correspondences

but first
wrote
"existence is
song"

should
have added
"and dance"

all this talk of transcendence
aside
isn't it true that
as utilitarian
commodity
poetry provides
a kind of colorful
billboard behind
which the actual
existential
landscape, with
its dry
arroyos
of misery
and its pocket
canyons of
distraction,
is so carefully
hidden?

Loop

The ego is
perfectly
able
to become aware
of the chance
it has
to leave
the realm
of self
preservation
behind
but this
ability
alone
does not
suffice
to realize
that chance
and what
you get
instead
is just
what happens
night
after night

Social Limits

A society that teaches
its members
never to think
beyond themselves
has good reason:
something
out there
beyond the
range
of the firelight
that makes
the animals uneasy
at night

Mundus vult
decipi

People want to be
deceived
not because
they want to remain
ignorant
but
because they know
the truth

Too Late for Pastoral

The real work
in life
is not this untenured
submissive
beating after
nickels
in the asphalt canyons

It's thinking
about what happens
to existence
out past
the limits
of its conditioning

Out there
in those once wide
familiar pastures
that get more distant
and narrow
every day

It's too late for pastoral
the cattle are headed
scared and
adrenalized
down tight channels
toward
an iron fence

Fear of Fear

The beasts are at pasture, the sun warms
the rocks. Night lingers in the wings.
It will rush forward, with its star-play,
Snowflakes scattered across oceans of ink,
the world will totter with its energy;
then calm will return, and thought will stop.

There is a vital damage which it is to
exist. There is a pressure of distance
and a tension of specialization
and a technological impairment
a denser air surrounds the enclosure
wall, beyond lies reality compact as lead.

One who longs to have lived but was forever
co-opted by the system now experiences
the first signal of a pensum in his center
and feeling same, steps forth into a day
whose grey light is shot through with rose
admittedly, but the rose is itself shot with grey.

Identification Tags

Ghosts do wear sheets but not for sleeping.

Sometimes people die while still alive
and then come back to life
but only partially. You can read the signs
around the eyes, which get
a dusty look like burned out hundred watt bulbs.

When they pass one another on the streets
there is a soft noise, as of muslin touching.

Sinking

Four hours after surgery
the slight pink floral pool
fills up with cool cement
that forms the head end
of a sledgehammer god
swings from the heels
to smash every waterlily
he ever made.

And when he's through
he sits down and weeps
tears of pity for this
universe he wishes
he never invented.

And the tears slosh
like waves over the
sides of a boat that
floats through the dark
parts of the sky.

And when it sinks
everybody can relax
at last, and go home.

Time

Time has curious way
of forgetting what's inside
decimated kisser
in-head computer's
down mouth opens
out come long slow
no thought trains

Small Change

Sense life's
expense of spirit
in a waste of shame's
oh maybe fifteen cents

and can't spare it—
ah lighten up, it happens
without spending experience
value doesn't apply

Orpheus out of Gas

Everything is done to pay off a debt one never incurred
That is why the mouth feels dry as if you were breathless
After a long climb at an altitude so high
When he opens his mouth to sing I can't hear a word

In the distance something crossing the
Bleak plain the inanimate culture of the future

Something like an insect or fly crossing
An endless wasteland
Littered with
The husks of some huge prehistoric beings
Whose itch to mutate became so powerful they chose
To shed their skins
Before they'd learned
That you need a skin to get across the desert

The Eleven O'Clock News

A pathetic race men have achieved malls and marinas
But never that state the Greeks called *ataraxia*
An imperturbability about death and life
Which should have been their sole aim in living.

Instead they're still trying to sink their teeth
Into the world, like the banqueter who eats up the mansion.
Big cities will simply be torn to pieces in those teeth
And nothing of value will come after them.

San Francisco will fall, New York. In fact when the picture starts
        to dissolve
I myself probably won't have the energy to leave my chair, here
        in the smoke
Ringed cities, in the dead wind that always blows
Far from where the happy suburbs and marinas are.

Anti-Solar

There's a certain melody in
everything   even this Sweden
of the soul
            in which I've chosen
                              to live
The music's
          too frigid   to pass
across the glass veranda
without creating an ice forest
out of its accreted crystals
the notes are like snake eyes on dice
unfortunate propositions
precipitated out of the atmosphere
of the cold side of the sun

Haunt

The soul mansion was shut down
and boarded up by some
program coordinator or other

Rarely does a living visitor get
past the Keep Out sign
as far as its broken gate
or the uncertain front steps

Alone and unlit
it stands as an object lesson
like some thunderstruck lover out of Ovid
up there on its Edward Gorey hill
reminding us
that the burning house of love grows dark
as soon as it's administered
by powers named Control

No light will shine into it
unless it shines in through
the keyhole of redemption

Drift

Under the dark top of the hill where
the wind blows she stands on one foot
scraping the mud out of her shoes
with a switch she picked up.

The hill is the sediment of the great
ice which returned earth
to earth ripped up and carried ten
thousand years in a napkin layer of drift.

Her light body walks uphill and stays
out ahead of me with her eyes open
into it and after her climbs the man
the dust whisking off her sleeve lights up the drift to.

Belief

Belief is consolation. But
what is there to believe?
The body moves, yet
before it comes to rest
it fails, and coming apart
pulls out of kilter
the body next to it
and under all this
the stars and gases
continue to whirl as
if disinterestedness
were not only not evil
but an actual blessing,
for thus something exists
after we do. One
cannot pull nothing
out of nothingness.
That said, one also
knows the order
of rotating bodies
is based on their
constant desire to
be at rest. And soon
enough they will be.
Inevitability may
not be pleasant but
it is the instrument of
the truth.

Here

Inevitability may not be pleasant but it is
the instrument of the truth
That is the message time writes
on the other side of the glass
through which we see darkly
in the two dollar toy-Tao of the videotape
that great moment in *Blade Runner* where Roy
Batty, expiring, talks about how everything
he's seen will die with him—
ships on fire off the shoulder of Orion
sea-beams glittering before the Tannhauser gates.

Memory is like molten gold
   burning its way through the skin
It stops there.
              There is no transfer
Nothing I have seen
will be remembered
beyond me
That merciful cleaning
of the windows of creation
will be an excellent thing
my interests notwithstanding.

But then again I've never been
   near Orion, or the Tannhauser
gates,

I've only been here.

Disordered Ideas

Some apparitions
can't help making
history stand still
and stop unfolding
its old accordion
medley of hopes
and meanings

The way the edges
of lit clouds appear
to give lightning a strange
duration
as it breaks across the sky
or the way
being propped up by
the crutch of an oak
seems to keep the sun
from going down
and thereby forgiving
everything

A CITIZEN OF THE FUTURE

"I know people will say of me, 'He was a maniac.' If this age goes down to posterity, understanding my mania will go down with it. The age will provide the background for manic tendencies. But what I should like is for people one day to say, 'He was a *moderate* maniac.'"

—*Bertolt Brecht, 1938*

Pressures of the Assembly Line

Question
when does a mere
slice of
human behavior
take on the compression
formality
and impact
of a work of art

Answer
when it becomes visible
against the flat backdrop
of history
with the clarity
of (say)
the sky-arc
of a bird in flight
over water
around twilight on
some perfect
summer night

Maybe some night
in Appalachia
with plant whistles
lonesome
in the red-sky
distance

Take the behavior on March 16 1985
of Mansel (Sonny) Hamlett
a man of 39

who worked in
a glass factory
in southwestern Pennsylvania

Sonny was a quiet
competent
reclusive worker
known mostly for being
very protective of his wife

They worked the same
afternoon shift
in the giant
Anchor Glass plant

Sonny made
nine dollars an hour
loading crates
of glass bottles
on wooden pallets
the kind that look
a little like the decks
of ships
that wash up in pieces
on beaches

Sonny's job was
both routine
and difficult

You didn't just
lift and toss
you had to pick
up each crate
of bottles
with the care you'd
use in holding
a newborn baby

and as delicately
lay it back
down again

The crates weighed
over a hundred
pounds apiece
there was a precise
and demanding
quota
of repetitious lifts
to be performed
like others
in his department
Sonny worked
under ever
vigilant eyes
of efficiency
analysts
foremen and
supervisors
seven days
twenty-four
hours
Anchor
produced glass
bottles for soda
beer
whiskey
and baby food

The strain
on Sonny
caused by
nonstop
on-the-job
pressure
to exceed

his mental
and physical
limits
resembled
in many respects
the stress on Anchor Glass
to overproduce
in an industry
doomed
by plastics
and
by foreign
competition

Like a canny dinosaur
that had survived
the ice age
but now faced
something
much worse
Anchor was one of those
few remaining
domestic
manufacturers
still trying to beat
the future
at its own game
two years earlier
the company
had been on the ropes
new owners
had brought in
efficiency experts
who'd instituted
quality controls
"speed-up"
production quotas
and stringent

disciplinary rules
the workload was huge
the pressure
on the workfloor
enormous

March 16
a Saturday morning
during her workbreak
Sonny Hamlett's wife
Judith
visited her husband
at the loading dock
he went on stacking crates
they talked
Sonny's foreman approached
Sonny and his wife
didn't notice
him at first
they were talking

Sonny's foreman
ordered her away

Not long into
the argument that ensued
the foreman called a supervisor
who suspended Sonny
on the spot
told him his job
might be lost
and sent him home

Instead of going home
Sonny left the plant
and went out
and bought
100 rounds

of ammunition
for his
.38
caliber
Smith & Wesson
handgun

What happened next
was prompted
by the moment

Sonny was
amok
in Amerika

He returned to Anchor Glass
in the Quality Control
office
he found
his foreman
standing there
before him

The foreman's name
was Donald Abbott
he was forty-eight years old

At the foreman's side
was Sonny's
supervisor
Paul Gabelt
a man of 52

Right there in Quality Control
Sonny shot them both
in their foreheads
fatally
then he stopped

to reload
his boots
lapped by
trickles of
managerial
level blood
the screens above
his head
reading out
Self-Destruct
the gadgetry shelves
lined with
video totems
looking down
angry but ineffectual
all around him

Sonny was ready
to stomp on down the hall
but then
his wife appeared suddenly
as if in a mist
out of nowhere
momentarily
breaking into
the Nicaraguan
Invasion
Killquake or
whatever it was had come over
Sonny's consciousness

She was screaming
Sonny saw only steam
before his eyes
he couldn't hear her
the god had laid a net
over him
it was not a net over lovers

he felt no love when
she threw her arms
around him

Judith
the human wife
couldn't stop him
at that moment
and no goddess
would step in to save
Sonny now
this mist closed
in around him

Sonny lived
in a weak society
he was its product
just as obviously as the
bottles in the crates
all around him
were products of Anchor Glass
but he was a strong man
at that moment
his rancor
was deep

Seeing
his wife
unable to break into his dream
his fellow workers
rushed up
and tried to get ahold of him
but he scattered them off
by firing some shots
over their heads
and walked on down the hall

He found the
department manager

Ralph Tumaro, 52
sitting in his office
the quality
control manager
John Coligan,
31
was sitting there too

Sonny killed
them both
in their swivel chairs
with single
shots
the cool
marksmanship
of chaos
was improving him
as a navigator
of his
own
fate
and also shot
in the chest
another supervisor
Richard Hosier, 38
who just happened
to be on hand
at the moment

Then he went
looking
for the plant
manager
his fellow
workers
yelling at him
in a weirdly
unintelligible

language
whenever
he looked
them
in the eyes
they
dove
for cover
Sonny was
isolated
out there
on the plateau
of his life

He'd created it for himself
he'd become an inventor of his
own form

He felt
godlike

The landscape
kept changing
as the moment
kept swelling
and expanding

Maybe in his
imagination
Sonny could feel
his cheekbones
being dusted
with that kind of
airbrush paint
meant to
simulate
coal-black
under the eyes

of heroes
in commando movies

He couldn't find
the plant manager

He came back
to the center
of the workfloor
where he'd been
stacking crates
of glass bottles
only a few hours
earlier
all around him now
the men
and women
he'd worked with
for years were yelling
strange things out at him

He trembled with fear
his legs shook
as he was pressing
the .38
against his chest
and pulling the trigger
he heard
the things they
were singing to him
not the
grateful praises
one would shower upon
a god
but instead the conflicted
and deeply
throat-twisted-inside-out
shouts of lamentation

that might be uttered by a child
witnessing
the murder of its parents
by its sibling

Sonny went out of the world
listening
to this mixed message
the apprehensive din
of a repressed
existence
at once
mourning
and castigating
itself

The next day
the plant was back
at full swing

Moment

Man talking to supervisor
conflicted gestures of submission
at odds with hate in eyes
through the eccentric surface
of what he seems to be saying
shines a hidden burden
the repressed suffering
of the alienated subject
who unconsciously expresses
the unreconciled nature
of real life
right here in the administrative hallway

Alice in Terminal Land

There's a small red fly
that swims into airless
administrative offices
through the screens
of video terminals
like a bloodshot eye
moving through the looking
glass backwards
a uniform light
that shines into the retina
from a Wonderland
whose prize is not
the expanding
of vision
but the sting
of disability glare

Brave New Work

Joysticks and trackballs
and light pens
may be used
the pen senses
the excitation
of the phosphors
activating
a cross hair
of visual feedback
and then
an optical mouse
rolls over
the touch screen
which is like a transparent
tablet
superimposed on the display
and activated by
the fingertip
of the numbed operator

A Citizen of the Future

stood on the synthetic turf
of the word processor college
and watched the creative writers
groove by with their programs
encased in gleaming digits
that will never develop blisters
and what he said to himself was
not included in this display

The System

These safety nets of ignorance
and inattention
woven out of the thin tissue
of printouts
are a life insurance policy
sold to a race without heirs

Shivering into the Future

If they can store
a human embryo
on ice for four days
in a lab
where's the surprise
when they freeze
a paycheck
for seven weeks
in a computer? The
death of emotion
was no immaculate
conception. Lenny
Tristano was 30
years ahead of
his time, the Birth
of the Cool
was a baby that
grew up like
Topsy on steroids,
and now we've got
a new cold mode
of delay
no other society's
ever equaled.

New Idol

The computer
which Thinking
has raised up
to the status
of its own equal
and to whose
greater glory
it's now intent
on eliminating itself

Technophilology

Antekna
Econics
Macronetix
Versatec

The computers clamp
the morphemes together
cold as metal limbs
of alien species
mating in space hangars

Epyx
Litronix
Compaq
Ambiset

Written on the edge
of word counter
"weight of neologism
not to exceed ten pounds"

Disotec
Versatronex
Dionex
Advantyx
Antekna

Technology

Technology is in its essence
a destiny within the history
of being and of the truth
of being, a truth that lies
in oblivion

An elemental experience
of what is world-historical
speaks out in it

And what is historical
falls through space senselessly
until it lands with a dead
clunk in nothingness

If you listen very closely
you'll hear the impact
more than 2000 times
every second

The Invention of Printing

Punching
the cold
hard metal
into the
soft
hot
metal,
Johnny
Gutenberg
invented movable
type

It was a trick
like Stukas
over bedrock
the way man's
violence to create
often
breaks into
history

Much as a guy
bending a crowbar
in a sideshow
changes the
whole shape
of attention
in the circus
for the next
50 decades

Then came Captain Video
and bent it back

Printing and History

The dusty volume opens
with a noise like wings beating
as a whole flock
of forgotten words
flutters out . . .

        A pack
of "technical writers"
meticulous, neo-erudite
and exact in their craft
may have their hands on
certain efficient power tools
the pulverizers of discourse
but I'd rather hold
a loud bag of dust
that once had a thought
impacted on it
than hear the continuous
noise of nothing

Reading the Technical Journals

The linguistic skil
saw of the contemporary
academic manual,
a drone of interact
and interface
somehow more faceless
and inactive
than Death itself,
threatens nothing
more than whatever's
left of Sense.
A yellowjacket at least
deposits its stinger in
its victim, then goes off to die
expressing a justice in nature
that no longer applies:
for having injected you with
their toxic load, *these*
drones shuffle off to get promoted.

Looking for Work in Teaching

I swallowed my pride
filed my heart away in the bottom
of the drawer
put my imagination
on the back burner
and covered all the openings
of my soul with spackle,
plaster and electrical tape

Then I sat down with
the MLA and AWP
job guides and found out
that unless I could quickly develop
a strong background in the
instruction of remedial English
composition to lefthanded
Icelandic women with green eyes
I might as well forget it

Teflon and Velcro

To get ahead
in this world of ours
you've got to have
a hide as tough
& a head as hard
as Teflon
and in addition
you've got to know
how to hook into
the powers that be
as perfectly
as though they and you
were matching slabs
of Velcro

Seeking Work and/or Permits in Berkeley

There are rows
of ringing desks
full of pastel phones
to be put cheerfully on hold.
There are, again, the wrong
clothes
on the seeker of light
privilege. And
there is public behavior
that is a tourniquet
of courtesy, applied
as a prelude to the anvil
of official regulation.

Being

a magnet for strange telephone calls
can be dangerous
all that energy pulled in through the wire
may create a negative polarization
in your soul
when the rapid switching of messages
gets too intense
you will be turned inside out
there will be a flash and puff of smoke
all those overloaded circuits shorting
a shower of sparks leaving a smell of sulfur
where you were there is nothing but empty space
and over this sudden vacuum there falls
a soft black curtain of silence
torn open
by the ringing of the phone

Glassitude

Silence is a distillate of noise.
Beneath the power saws and the Van Halen
Tapes of the neighbors a tiny
Island of quiet is deposited
An oasis of reflection leached out
Of the gross drone of the bourgeoisie . . .
Still between us and the futureway
Lies only the heavy-heavy
Metal kids' halfway house
And when Billie Holiday tries to sing into
The two hundred decibel incisors
Of their exploding mechanical tools
Forget it sister!
It's a case of monkey see monkey do
Multiplied by the potential
Hopelessness of forever

At the end of the hominid
Chain a grey sediment of tension
Quietly accumulates like a trace
Element. The miracle of any reflection
Leached out of the gross drone
Of the bourgeoisie shouldn't tempt one
To forget that out there on the
Interpersonal frontier Tab A
Meets Slot B for purposes of Insert
To exactly that tune.
Whereas:
In the universe of glass I dream
(Which is actually made of icy words)
The glass boat that floats in

A glass pool to the musical
Silence of a glass étude . . .
Is absolutely unheard.

5 P.M.

A seam opens
in the traffic
flow I
hear this
mockingbird in my
backyard
and when it's gone
Satie
played by
Shearing
on an antique FM
drifting
down through yellow plum
leaves
against the blue rush
hour sky

2 A.M.

On the freeway feeder
listening to
the thoughts
of the crickets
isn't easy

In the Wet

November rain spins down on the industrial
Eyewash of the Nimitz
Endless headlight fish slip upstream through it

At a quarter to midnight the human race
After splashing through the yellow pages
Gets a brain made on an emergency basis

But it won't fit into the door
Of the world we locked ourselves out of
We won't be aound to operate it anymore

Now very different things will go on in there
Like things that go on
In a car plunging slowly down through a body of water

What you see is a film of the past rinsing the windshield
What you hear is a sound track of the past sluicing
In through the air vents, in the form of bubbles

Muffled Report

Sky goes dark to the east
getting ready to rain again
you leave those curtains open
and let the last light
of day drain in
there may be no more later
ideas of contingent fate
flat grey in the low blue
landscape of house tops
sinking through trees to bay
it is more difficult to say
anything through the medium
of each instant as it drips
through the day's dropper
than it is to lift the full spoon
to the flame of your heart
where it creates this backfire

Commuting

The humiliation of being
constantly observed
by a hostile or derisive eye
is certainly no joke
but neither is
not being able to find
your shoes

The rich buy
themselves out of it

The bus
plunges through the rain
a full load
of long faces
stares out the window
into the historical ontology
of itself

At Spieker Pool

Time goes on and on and on
Life never stops for one minute
It rains then the rain stops
I take my heart for a ride on the bus
It gets lost
I find my goggles
Sunk into lassitude
I drink coffee
Out of a thermos
A normal man
White weak and slow
I set out
Hoping for open spaces to know
So I can see what's appropriate
To life
If only its lower reaches
Instead I get off
And find myself inside
Tall stone portals
Momentarily blinded
By bronze torsos rippling in sun
And turquoise chlorine
There for an hour
I'm permitted to go
Up and down
Under the sign that says
Is It Tough Enough?
In brief proximity with the divine
Ones
Allowed
To move through their blue
And golden air

Whose being
Roars and tumbles
Enjoying itself in the waves
As I have never done
Privileged though I am
To share the liberty of
Their Aether
A radiance
At once deadening and immortal

Locker Room at Harmon Gym

All healthy young
american men want is
to fuck and get money
but when you take
showers with them they
look big and pink and
funny. They have
serious looks on their
faces. You must not meet
their eyes as they
soap their special
little balls and penises.
They are here because
money can buy all this.

There are five hair blowers
in the locker room.
Four of them
are really machines.
And the other one goes
out and gets in the
green water. He swims up
and down in the
fuzzy nighttime neon
under the big egyptian
stone block buildings and
under water everyone wears
goggles; sounds seem
to come from far away.
Bubbles come out of their
noses. They are really machines.

Autumn on the Campus

Patches of sparse hair
on the otherwise
bald head
of the statue
flicker in the sun.
Past walk
two teenagers
with brutal faces.
One mumbles something.
The other says, "really."
Amid scattered leaves
the light melts
on the pavement
like ice cream.
The poets are dead,
the wine-drinker's head
topples in his
lap. True, the gods are
still living, but above,
in a world
we know nothing of.

Moonrise on the Street of Futons

Here on Solano
where the northside
Berkeley money
comes
to make its peace
with the cash registers
of Albany
the moon rises
above the futon store

Pale ball of oblivion
she moves the world
out of the blue landscape
of the night she's part
of the will of God
his clear eye
that roundly gazes into
the dark sky
like a hole
cut through deep blackness
into an ivory universe

Hanging over the Aegean
she is the same cool
pale source
that once fell like rain
to wash clean
the songs
of Homeric singers

But here in Albany
she is reduced to

a dry
slice of white
greek cheese
stuck with rubber cement
to the orange night sky
over the capuccino bar

Thinking About Pound on Shattuck Avenue

Thinking about Pound on Shattuck Avenue
is like genuflecting in hiking boots
a classic case of being overequipped.
If we live in a sea of insincerity, as they say,
how many additional drops
does it take to make a wave?
Forlorn as driftwood, *The
ABC of Reading*
sits untouched, swamped
by enough *Chez Panisse*
to give Neptune a heartburn.

At the brink of the frankly autobiographical
one hesitates. Can one live with grace
in such a place? Is escape possible?
were my thoughts of the day
So what else is new . . .
A clerk looked my way.

Art in our time is a toy of the middle
class, I said, squirming in
my bike pants in the pasta maker
bookshop. Gourmets fidgeted
all around me, eyes glued
to the pages of the Rilke cookbooks.
Under the effete weight
the hardwood floors contracted.
Death came very near.
It is really all around us,
a pang of dissonance hidden
in the surreptitious music of the cash register,
in the timid squeak of earth shoes,

behind the piped Sibelius—
pitched much too low for dogs to hear,
the melody of the death
of culture. The poets are dead.
Ezra floated home on a boat
of flowers
just in time.

Shattuckworld

If it's not true that
art has become a trained poodle
of the techno social elite
then how do you explain
Wayne Thiebaud's oils of pastry in *The Chez
Panisse Dessert Cookbook*? a coming together of art
as culturescape and food-as-meaning-of-life
into a chocolate cream pie of kitsch
of which each consumer will get an equal slice

Éclair

Mist rising from the
mixed postindustrial landscape

into long bluish tubular clouds
on an intense pink backdrop—

one of those wayne thiebaud
custard pie suns rising

over the little vine covered
grotto advertising tonight's menu

If eating is the repression of food
remember after all

the triumph of the individual
is never anything but the triumph of the will

to subjugate other existents
to one's body

The Age of Cain Diet

I'm looking for the joke
with a microscope
I don't wanna be your dog
you gods of eternity
but I also don't want
you to use my head
for an ashtray
a faceful of burning rubber
isn't my idea
of graceful ageing

But the structural habits
of a homicidal society
have nothing to do with grace
I think as I descend Shattuck
on my banged-up Univega
unnoticed in the aggressive stream
of upscale metal-navigators
propelled by strong tides
of an urgency to purchase
with plastic

It's up to them
to either avoid me
or to have to put up with
seeing me on the menu someday
another pimento splash
on the gentrifacted asphalt

The rich would eat the poor
if it were legal and the
poor tasted better

As for me
very little fat left
on the old bones
but a high fibre content
like gristly pasta
might just interest
these anorexic consumers

After all wasn't
anthropophagy the original
gourmet sport

Yuppieworld

The last
wave of human
behavior flashing
up on the
terminal shore
with the light
click and sheen
of plastic
cards touching

Democracy

In the motel
room mirror

a yellow
light pulses

on polyester lips
pressed to sandwiches of hair

Northwest 157

Upper prairie corporate
technology Friday
commuter dinner flight
3 M and Honey
well clones fly
home to San Diego
Tokyo over scotch
on the rocks it's audits
comptrollers all that
money talk
intimate and smooth
as aluminum
until plane hits a few
upslope pockets
over Denver "Like
another drink?" "You
talked me into
it honey" and then
the laughter gets harder
edged the drinks sway
and rock on the
plastic trays
the Sunbelt seems
far away finally
all that liquor
locks in they
nod off into light
troubled slumber
at last the strange
peace of heavy
lateral turbulence only
disappointing thing's
we don't go down

United 524

Violence against nature
is ultra mundane.
On the jet plane no one
grumbles when
put through experiences an ape
couldn't tolerate without
a half pint of librium
shot direct into the vein
That's called being civilized
It's supposedly an advance
on that hominid state
wherein one does
what one's instincts dictate.
Instincts are dead. What's
left is the binary dictum
keep your mouth shut and let
your nervous system mutate
or keep your mouth shut
and let your nervous system
steep in a martini cracked
out of a can. On airplanes
businessmen never talk to me
and I never sit next to
anybody else.

Commuter Flight

The calm interior secret
cuddled into the self
like a consoled infant
the knowledge of death
it doesn't matter what
they say it's what they
are by which we know
them. The businessmen
get the drinks under
their belts and tell each
other their life stories
stressing the career
and finance details
but through it comes
like water through a
sieve the long denied
truth of being which
doesn't resemble what
they say at all.

Over the Eastern Slope

Seeing earth
vertebrae
as piano keys
from five miles up

puffy oyster tofu colored cloud
drifts in tufts above
snow ranges of the Great Divide
like touch

typing
soft white fingers playing Bach
on the spine
of the continent

The Engine Nacelles of a DC-10
Seen as Signals of the
Double Meaning of Existence

I believe in
a radiance that shines out from
the literal beauty of the truth
as from metal wings shaken
in the sun

but I also believe
in the irresistible undertow
created by a current
that pulls very deeply
from an entirely
different dimension
where everything is true
and yet there is
no light at all

Free Fall

Self-infolded we feel a false footing
under us is the ground and then
when it's pulled away and we begin to
fall toward a bottom that isn't there
we want to know what's happening but
the fast air as it goes by in this elevator
shaft of last chances we're dropping
through seals up the lips before
they can form around the question

Going Over

a person drops
down
on a wire
depending
from the sky
he can't secrete
a filament
like a spider
but he can hear
a jungle telegraph
without a wire
on a sony
he can
hang on
to the guy
rope of a
conditional
existence
on a peninsula
that creeps
out into the
cold steam
of an archipelago
but he can't
climb back up
because the
tensile strength
of the platinum
remains less
than the hydro
dynamic power
of the falls

Legacy

We're all going to
so we might as well face it
first turn to powder
then blow away
from the material dimension completely
and the day that comes true
the things we own
will remain here in the world
laughing at us with the hyena mouths
of everything we have
most feared in this Theatre of Blurs

Untying

One who's untied
all the knots cut all
the cords disengaged
all the hooks and claws
of the stuff of this world
gets (so they say) a very
empty feeling deep inside
like a bowl seeking some
perfect fluid   hollow yet
very beautiful and soothing
smooth and curving
and soon filled up
with the nectar of vacuity

Oiling the Stars

Quiet starry night
No creaking noises coming from the direction of Betelgeuse
Or Sirius
The working parts of those big silent running gearboxes
Are lubricated by
Transdimensional existence vaseline
A gelatin lubricant made from pulverized cartilage
Of human beings
Who don't know
That though they dry up when they die
Their body oils and fluids
Get a whole new use
Greasing the stiff joints
Of the universe

Thrall

Close your eyes and listen
to the hum of the dead
under the ground as well
as that of the yet unborn
still planted deep in the future
a kind of anthem or hymn
that works on us like a spell
keeping us in the eternal
breath-thrall of the living

HOW IT GOES

Puffing her cheeks, she blew a jet of smoke ... the smoke moved around in circles, floating on air currents ... Backlit, her face looked lunar and cold, taking on a bloodless patina, like cheese or milk ... The tiny mound of powder on the table resembled a pyramid shorn of its apex by some levelling blade ... "Someday," she said, "fate or some ... some mysterious ... some *force* ... can put the finger on you or me ... for no reason at all ... and all it takes is that little touch to knock you off your course ... and steer you onto another road ... a road that heads down and down and down ... and there's nothing you or me can do about it ..." She looked out the window through the shaggy palm trees into the parking lot, where someone was gunning the engine of a Porsche ... Fog enclosed the hotel complex in a cobwebby silence like a forest from which each inhabited bungalow stood out like an isolated plantation, the last outpost of a previous civilization which might never again return ...

Dripping with sweat, tense and exhausted after two hours of maneuvering through traffic on the freeway, he walked into the room where his lover waited with another man, and smiled grimly at them, and ejected a small dry laugh that spoke of a carefully measured hatred . . . "All I care about," he said, "is breaking you two down into pieces so small they'll be able to paint the walls with them . . . I want it to be a painting of death . . . the colors will be white and grey, from your bones . . . and dark brown and red, from your blood . . . it'll be a beautiful painting, violent but beautiful, like life . . ."

1 a.m. in the Valley: the man bent over the bar was either crying or laughing or choking . . . or perhaps all three at once . . . a strange ululating sound emerged from his throat . . . then after awhile he was quiet, and sipped his drink . . . and softly began speaking, to no one in particular: "They told me she was as sweet and nice . . . as the girl next door . . ." he sipped again, then paused, staring up into the hazy barnlike darkness of the ceiling . . . "but once I got to know her she seemed like . . . more like something they serve at the Ritz . . . that's been laying out in the sun too long . . ." Without looking at him, the bartender came by and with a gliding motion wiped the bar clean, sweeping a folded white towel over its polished surface . . .

The man paced back and forth, gesturing with his hands as he spoke . . . "It's like a neon sign flashing on and off . . . It's like clouds passing in front of the moon, bathing things in cool, pure white light . . . and then the next minute in thick dark shadow . . . Good and evil can change places like that, real quick and without reason or meaning or notice . . ." "And there's nothing," the woman said, "that you or me can do about it . . ."

The apartment was hot and airless and the night seemed to go on forever . . . Cars roared back and forth beyond the curtained windows . . . "Nobody comes," she said, tapping her nails nervously on the dark, stained wood of the table before her, "nobody cares . . . somewhere out there a lot of talking goes on . . . it's always gone on, it's still not about anything, and none of it matters . . . just a lot of noise on a little ball spinning through empty space . . . and headed nowhere in one hell of a hurry . . ." "You go on talking like that," the man in the bathrobe said to her, "and somebody *will* come . . . they'll come for *you* . . ."

He was leaning against the refrigerator, staring down at her with the look of a man who's got something on his mind that he doesn't want to say . . . "Maybe you love me and maybe I love you . . . Maybe somebody's gonna take the fall, and maybe somebody's gonna end up on their feet . . ." "I'll give you two more maybes," she said . . . "Maybe we're sitting here in this kitchen in the middle of the night and nobody knows we're here but some monitoring device a million miles out in space where disks of gas a billion times the size of the sun are rotating faster than the speed of light . . . and maybe what the monitoring device is saying to itself is, 'you hear that? he's just handing her another line . . .' "

"Never get crowded into a corner," the man said to his friend, "never let them get too close . . . always keep one face turned away, even when the other one's turned toward them . . ." "But who are they?" "You'll know them . . ." His friend nodded: "I already do . . ." He sat motionless at the wheel as the light changed . . . On both sides, cars began to move . . .

His shirt was soiled, the collar torn, he needed a shave, a trickle of sweat inched down toward his brow over the wrinkled corduroy of his forehead . . . "I feel all dead inside . . . I'm backed up in a dark corner and I don't know who's hitting me . . . It's like I'm in a bad dream, only I know I'm not, because if I was, this is the part where I'd wake myself up . . . but I can't . . . I don't even feel like trying . . ." His voice tailed off and he went on sitting in front of the television in silence . . . on the screen before him, Grand Prix race cars negotiated difficult corners in the rain . . . at his side was a table holding a metal tray on which the half-eaten remains of a Mexican dinner waited to be thrown away . . .

The two women sit quietly at a table, watching light rain fall steadily in the street outside . . . one of them stretches and yawns . . . the other glances at her briefly, then goes back to staring out the window . . . anything could happen here, at any moment . . . but nothing will . . .

She didn't like being alone with him . . . the tension around him was a palpable force, like gravity . . . She shrank back from him, as someone might from a vicious animal . . . he didn't seem to notice . . . "From the start," he said, "it all went one way, you know that? It was in the cards . . . or it was fate or a jinx, or whatever you want to call it . . . I never cared about the money . . . all I wanted was you . . . I walked the streets of strange cities saying your name . . . Why are you looking at me like that?" "Because I'm afraid . . ."

"That's just how it goes," the black-haired waitress says . . . "Every night it's the same . . . he comes in, sips his coffee, plays the same song on the jukebox . . . a real sad, slow one . . . then he leaves . . . where he goes, we got no idea . . . and then one night he doesn't come in . . . or the next one either . . . it's the last anybody sees of him . . . never even told us his name . . . and we never asked . . . that's just how it goes, I guess . . ." Two or three guys in booths around the room nod silently in agreement . . . The clock on the wall points its hands into a space that keeps on going long after closing time . . . out and out and out . . . into the endless night . . .

They stood on a street corner in the winter sun, talking about the tenor of the times . . . One was smoking, the other was rubbing his own arms, like someone trying to keep warm . . . the one who was smoking was doing most of the talking . . . "Some days, you know, it's like life just charges in on you like a crazy dog loose off its leash, wanting to take a bite out of your heart if you'll let it . . . you just can't give it the chance, man . . . a minute later it's just as likely to change its mind and start coming on as friendly as a puppy . . . I'm not knocking it, man, I'm just trying to understand it . . ."

They met in a bar . . . She'd known him about two weeks when he suddenly dropped the boom on her . . . the shock was enormous . . . his hatred staggered her . . . She couldn't figure it out . . . What made him want to do such a thing? "Why'd you single me out?" she asked him . . . "Because I can't get everyone," he said . . .

The weights and values of liquids and solids never varied their proportions, rents and prices rose and fell, humans were born and died, the sun rose over the city the same way every morning, the sun went down over the city the same way every night ... The days stacked up on top of the days and the weeks stacked up on top of the weeks and the months stacked up on top of the months and the years stacked up on top of the years, until the man couldn't see over them anymore ... "And then I came out here ... here you don't notice the time going by because there's nobody around to remind you of it ... nobody around at all ..."

Men and women were born to die but never more so than in this age in which a certain silent war has gone on for years . . . Toward the end of it a woman who chain-smoked, who lived in a mobile home park where the air had the greenish tinge of ancient brass, who'd considered selling one of her kidneys to get money for food, whose husband wore the same grey undershirt every day, who never left her modest home, suddenly realized she'd become a zombie in reverse . . . the world was dead and she was living . . . but no one noticed . . . not one living soul . . .

They stared at each other across the formica table top . . . He cleared his throat: "Vengeance is mine . . . saith the Lord . . ." She laughed nervously . . . "What do you suppose He meant by that?" "I think He meant that since it was Him that made you, it was likewise Him that could take you apart . . ." "I don't find that real consoling . . ." "I don't guess you were meant to . . ." She laughed quickly again, then looked away . . .

She tried to talk but no words came . . . The doctor smiled at her kindly . . . She cleared her throat and began again . . . "I don't know how to explain it . . . I feel so damn sad . . . nothing makes me happy . . . what's wrong with me, doctor? I can't keep my mind on anything . . . can't concentrate at all . . . don't feel like going around people . . . feel like I'm not worth a damn . . . like I did everything wrong . . . like I'm going to die . . . or worse . . . like everybody in the world's dead already . . . they're all dead people . . . it gets that bad sometimes . . . doesn't make sense to live . . . like there's nothing I can do . . . might as well put an end to it all . . . but then I guess a lot of it really just depends upon sales . . . I had a really lousy month last month . . . the market's really bad . . . you know?"

If you ripped the fronts off the houses you'd find animals, eating, drinking, sniffing each other, trying to conceal from each other the fact that they're merely animals, drifting through life, building big structures of nothing on top of their animal lives, which add up to nothing, only fuel, fuel for eternity, where the billions of the quick and the dead, the trillions of dead, swim around in convulsive circles, howling, gasping, rattling, adding their small reflexive cries to the grand cyclic howling of the dead, lost universe . . .

WHITE MONKEYS

Arcadia

A rapid triphammer sequence of percussive events in shimmering treble rhythms announces the day of radiance which was promised in the earliest books like speeded-up Monet paintings growing inside the half-life of a Balinese gong-tone. Light breaks over the glass arcades splitting into a hundred facets each reflecting some slight movement of the lagoon whose surface is marked with the spore-like circles and ovals of half-submerged water lilies clustered together in schools. Some boys are tapping small brass drums with wooden mallets at a pace so fast you can't even see their hands moving. On their faces are expressions of rapt, serene concentration.

Cinderella

A moon the color of a white bone lying on blue snow slowly
floats up a moving stairway to the stars, rescuing the sadly vic-
timized word "escalation" from its bleak political context and
suggesting that, given the chance, even such ugly duckling ter-
minology can turn heads. The beautification of terms by con-
text is a Cinderella story that tells us something about language,
how it uses its terms in a floating manner. The words waver
according to their weightiness. The heaviest expressions wob-
ble like sumo wrestlers on a tightrope thin as a platinum diode,
whereas the lightest ones glide so smoothly that their unwaver-
ing course across the clear landscape of the summer night leaves
no questions to be asked, no mysteries to be discovered. These
sylphlike apparitions seem to achieve a perfect aerobic
denomination of truth, but it's an illusion: a glass slipper can't
be danced in. Cinderella skates hopefully over the polished land-
scape of the ballroom floor, but we see through her as easily as
though the rayon and cellophane of her dress were spun from
the tissues of a transparent soul. As the night deepens, she
climbs out of that cheap dimestore gown and slips into the
pool — where amid the buoys and innertubes she becomes beauti-
ful, Prince Charming or no Prince Charming, because I have
willed it.

Frontier

As the car hurtled silently along the black road into the huge
darkness of the November countryside the diminishing strip of
asphalt ahead made an inverted V that kept pouring toward us
like black water from a hose connected to a great pump located
somewhere in the future. Inside the mechanical tide of that thin
strip it was possible to feel the planet spinning as eternity reeled
it in then tossed it back with the gesture of a fisherman throw-
ing back a small fish.

The Anarchist

When it got dark, a girl began to sing. She sang in Russian, and, with the wind sighing in the trees as accompaniment, it sounded very sad. A chill crept up the lawn from the lake, where a mist had started to rise off the water, creating green, blue and red halos around the lanterns of the piers. Across the lake lights danced in the windows of the big estates. Stars gleamed overhead, notes on the musical score of the dark. When the wind went through the trees it made a sound like the strumming of a vast harp. Suddenly the girl stopped singing. The night crouched on all fours, poised to spring; then a clear peal of laughter rang out.

Cheating

One wants to be able to reach out without looking and touch death lightly on the shoulder—but when one's hand encounters something cold and alien in the dark, like a touch of the marble statue's arm, with bits of loam still clinging to it, one draws back, realizing this is not the way.

Core Sample

The permanent overtaxing pressure to adjust to the administered world leaves people neither time nor strength to do anything but bore deeper into the material clay of their lives — as though their destiny had been to turn into drill-bits, moving vertically downwards forever, scooping out protracted autobiographies in the form of core samples, tapes, video records. The important questions met along the way are drowned out by the roar of the earthworms.

Nobody There

One of the bonuses of living along the interdimensional rift zone of a society caught between its future in the age of electronic magic and its past in the spellcasting of the caves is the hang-up phone call, wherein, for a few seconds, one hears the heavy breathing of eternity — followed by an abrupt click, as the other world breaks contact.

White Monkeys

The greatest possibility open to us lies in giving ourselves up. But the mere thought of giving ourselves up is followed by an inward shudder. Fear immediately freezes everything into a stylized, discrete paralysis, like those isolated moments, laid end to end, in which Zeno's arrow tries to cross the sky. Since Zeno's arrow exists only inside his paradox, it can never land, and since after thinking about giving ourselves up, we too begin to take on the immateriality of a logical demonstration, it makes more sense to think of white monkeys fading back into the white paper on which they are painted — or of the final note in a piece of music. When its ripples ebb away and there is no hint of reverberation left anywhere, silence fills the room; not the cold silence of a paradox but the warm silence of a white opal chip slipping downward through a viscous fluid inside a black glass jar. The opposite of this silence is music itself. Music is a dream without the isolation of sleep, in which it appears we're meant to endure life on a dying planet by becoming aware of emotion.

TOWARD A THEORY OF BEAUTY

Voodoo Macbeth

Works of art are set in motion by patient contemplating. This goes to show that they are truly after-images, in our thing-bound age, of prehistorical shudders, bringing back the terror of the primal world and thrusting it up against a contemporary backdrop—like spiritual manna descending in front of a billboard for beauty products. Huts, fronds, palm trunks slowly come into focus in dawn's gradual miracle of apparition.

The boat is docking at a makeshift harbor of bamboo pylons that jut out like disembodied cranes' legs from the muddy, tree-island-dotted stream. One can hear the drums of Macbeth sounding in the distant work of art. Arrows start falling on the deck of the boat.

Dawn Moon over Bay through Clouds
above Eucalyptus

As the eucalyptus tunes its colors for the day from deep green through silver I realize works of art are neutralized and qualitatively changed epiphanies, they are charged with the same intensity as apparitions in nature, but displaced across orders of experience from the literal to the virtual world.

Between five and six in the morning the soft blanket of dark unravels into a blue purple, then a violent grey scarf of light that hangs around solid things at first loosely, later snug like a glove, adhering and becoming part of a specific world.

Works of art collude with apparition in the way an apparition rises above people beyond the reach of their intention—beyond the reach also of the world of things. This quality of apparition sometimes makes works of art resemble gifts from the sky.

Suicide with Squirtgun

While apparition is the instant of illumination and of being touched by something, recording and preserving it is another trick entirely: turning this timeless moment into an aesthetic instant, which is something that has duration. This is no easy task, like trying to keep a firefly's glow in a bottle without the firefly.

The transcending element in works of art is something momentary. Their entry into time is always a tight squeeze requiring the shoehorn of an "art experience," which fits them into such-and-such temporal dimensions.

Works of art flower into images, which create instants out of mere moments. Then again, art is like a soft explosion, as when the hero in the German play kills himself with a squirtgun while standing under some tremendously dark and emotive trees, as the sadness of the river landscape in the backdrop announces the arrival of dusk in the valley.

There is a sigh from inside nature, as all the durations that have unfurled suddenly begin to fold themselves up—like huge petals closing.

Calving

Every expression is a falling silent, like the departure of the calved sections of a glacier into the flow of the surrounding ice. Music gains strength in its fading. A sound disengages itself from the others, then stops. This is the passage of art back into nature. At dusk the tree trunks cease to stand out from the dark Hopper-esque forest beyond, and once again the world disappears behind its veils of transcendence.

ANGELOLOGY

Angelic Witnesses

Bathed in a warm
celestial light
like young oak trees
sprung from the floor
of heaven
under jade green swags
of leaves
with coral fruit
on a backdrop
of lapis lazuli
blue as the veins
over a madonna's breast
these Piero
della Francesca angels
have choirboys'
soft ephebic faces
yet seem eternally wise
in their attention
the faint
hint of a smile
of thoughtful contemplation
curls the edges
of their oval mouths
they contemplate the mystery
with steady eyes
and no fear
of error or trickery
as if they could
make the world a radiant place
simply by witnessing it

Divine Dancers

for Edwin Denby

"The angels standing
two or three feet away
terrify,"
Edwin said
in a letter from New York
18 years ago.
At the time I supposed
that by "angels"
he meant
"beautiful young persons."
Lately though I've wondered
if the sense of grace
and presence
it takes
to recognize beauty
in persons
might not also enable one
to recognize
the Great Ones
when they sweep
across our sphere
of the universe
in a state of
presque vu—
almost seen
in the phantom
motion
of a curtain
stirred by no breeze—
hovering
behind a screen

waiting there
to manifest themselves
as Divine Dancers
to those gifted few
who've got eyes for them.

Three Little Words

Nasir K
circumscribed the
cosmological
mystery
in three little words
naming his angels
azal
azaliyat
and
azali

The Ipseity
of the first angel
is like an itch
you can't scratch

The second angel
sits under the azaleas
of heaven
sipping a mint julep

The third angel
is a retard
which thrusts
things back
into the cosmic
trash compactor

He is known as
The One Who
Makes Clean

Star Wars

If they throw up needles mirrors beams lasers
in a super noxious cloud as dense
as the eyebrows of Edward Teller
what will happen to the great
angels whose trajectories
all that space flak intersects?

What counter
technology can those loyal soul
partners of ours use to save
themselves from the sad blind
material beings whom they came
here to protect and guide?

Burst Phase

I dreamed I was in a green telephone booth
receiving 10^{18} watts
of energy from the sun
on the first day of World War 3

And in that dream I remembered you
you were orange bright
like a gold lamp hung in a dark green night

You expanded exponentially
and became a white enamel
coating everything

Angelology

There's a moment
  when you pass through
  your angel
  and become the creature
  not of the two
  but of the fact you are
  beyond any chance involved
  with another figure who is you

And the moment that you pass through
  you are then something
  that that angel was
  and no longer
  the thing that you are

Rip Chord

We were falling together for years through worlds
on the Trans Aether Express
when suddenly yet slowly you reached over me
to touch a sort of string that grew out of my
left clavicle and plucked it

When the white flower popped open over us
retarding our plummet into eternity
I felt the ganglia wilt
like tulips in a blizzard
all the way down to my kneecaps

Fear

Fear, like a Rube Goldberg tumbler doll, cannot be kept down
It keeps popping back up schmoolike to create
Personal hells through which you can't navigate
Without a benign partner at your right hand
One able if not to control those terrifying moments
Then to keep them at plume's length with
One adroit aileroning movement of a pinion

Stupor

The stupor of a single angel-prince
can be powerful enough to bring
an entire flock of sub-angels instantly
to its metaphysical knees
in a contagion of celestial paralysis
whose effects are felt on earth
some years later à la sunspots

Not droughts or floods follow
but a great spiritual inattention
spreading into the center of things
a psychic slowdown
a dumbness with no exit
a swelling of irrational fear
and the rise to power
of certain theories or parties
rooted in linked tautologies:
that *what is not visible does not exist*
and *we are all alone here*

Straight Up

I look around the sky's too deep here I get the bends I see
men in black suits fluttering around a white hot cash register
I burn my fingers on the coffee pot, Lord
you can't go fishing in a watermelon patch
you can't rollerskate in a buffalo herd
some illiterate bonzo standing outside the door of the temple
good for nothing but turning the prayer wheels
knows more than I do about how to be part of the conscious
    universe
you can't put a spiritually dead person among the living and
    expect to see breath on the mirror
you can't pull the wool over the eyes of eternity for very long
what goes around comes around and catches up with you
in the middle of your backswing
so that the club head clips you hard right upside the head
after that you feel a profound need to lie down
but the rules of the game say that now more than any
other time it is your duty and imperative to remain straight up

Artaud and the Angels

High on chloral hydrate
Artaud said: "I resemble the angels
in that they and I are made
of the same organic material
but I'm superior to them
because I know *it*
is not *me* — and this allows
me the luxury of being able to spit
on this carcass I inhabit, and which inhabits me."

His hatred of a body nailed to a wall of addiction
allowed him to leap out of it
into a form so much more fearful that
when he started to slip into the netless gulf of himself
not even his angel could catch him.

Artaud and the Angel after Mexico

He went to Mexico
He came back changed
He got off
the steamboat *Mexique*
at Saint-Nazaire
walked into
the Café du Dôme
still holding his valise
and began to retell
his adventures in the mountains

He seemed
extremely altered
prophetic
a little uneasy
exalted
and strange

His angel
just sat there
over the pernod
and shook her
pretty head

He wrote up his trip
for the papers
and spent the payment
on a rest cure
He kicked
his heroin
and cocaine
habits   He said

"I've got to clear my head"
He was ready
to begin
a great voyage
but he soon learned
that without drugs
he was so lucid
that his brain
became a silver chainsaw
into which his spine
was being fed

That's the thing
about a clear head
his angel told him

The Divine Comedy

Nel mezzo del cammin di nostra vita
Mi ritrovai per una selva oscura
Chè la diritta via era smarrita
I didn't know how to get to first base
I stared into the eyes of eighteen
year old girls like an escapee
from a spaceship   I forgot things
possessions   money   my name
missed appointments for job
interviews and sat for hours in airports
looking lost and forlorn as a deportee
I took the first plane out   I didn't
know where it was headed

It was headed here

Arc

It turns the corner
like a smoky plume
and runs out
to loop around
the dead moons of Jupiter

This street is named
the New Angel
after the one who
cut it through me

The angel who preferred to free men
by taking from them
rather than making them happy
by giving to them

Their frozen pinions are ice

Clouds are their concern for us
The angel's tear
falls through the clear ether
silently
and when it hits the earth's atmosphere
turns into mist

Scattered showers
occur when
among the lesser legions
strange fits of weeping
befall the protectors of men

Of their meteorological effects
the only other thing we know
is that snow is what happens
when they decide to lay
their earthly forms upon the ground

February

The plum blossoms tumble
down on the north
wind that pulls spring in
a light rider on the back
of winter. It doesn't
snow but the blizzard of
white plum petals is
memento of those
milliard angels in the Talmud
new ones each moment
in endless hosts created
to sing their hymns before God
faster than a fingersnap
then cease to exist
and pass into nothingness
on the wind of the sun.

Revelation

The Kreutzer sonata
settles on the snow
like ice on diamonds

In this moment
speechlessness,
rather than God,
appears

Bound

The same thing is to be thought of
and is the thought that it is

for you will not find thinking apart
from that which is

this has been bound by fate

like all other things
like this smoke

like those flowering green
things against the snow

they show that
fate and character coincide exactly

Transformational Propositions

Some kind of gods
move around in these propositions

They think that to be
and not to be
is the same thing
and not the same thing

It is
but it is not

It is not but possibly
it can be

It's like the story of
the god who
turning back to look at the smoke

eyed woman, steps
on his cape
and becomes a man.

Sexual Theory of History

King Arthur aboard Kon Tiki
swept Ophelia away
to a self made Atlantis

Their empire was his sails of silk
and her hull of skin
which cut a path right through him
like the prow of a drifting continent

Induction

lunar eyes of women
glide through the
    mental forest
stratified
  and scored
by what they've seen
      they
seem to have
the sensibility
  of the flayed

certain animals
can almost change
your idea of love
    by induction

Suspension

I behold you, lost in infinity with me,
and it makes me wonder

where the ground is
no longer visible

how to continue breathing in
this medium charged

with the question
that enters us every time we open our mouths

and get that little catch
in our throats, like having a bird there.

Angel Arcs

Individual lives
move along a curve
of which they comprise
isolated moments
which by themselves mean nothing
but the whole grand arc
has a shape
that might mean
everything
to someone standing
beyond the stars

After Dante

The sun draws
things it creates
into its arms, and
then crushes them
out of its surplus
of energy, which no
living thing can stand
for long. Still, heat
is life, to speak
is to be warm and
to be alive is to
make something clear
where nothing was.
The heart pumps
but also cuts
itself into pieces
for love. But what
is love if not
the sun, and yet
where does light go
when it streams
through the veins
out into the darkness
of the universe?

Circling Back to Earth

Flight plan changed last minute
first angel went off left me here
picking out phantom wing schemata in
stark empty armed plum tree traceries
this day Sunday morning the world "dank"
out there she'd said yet "warm" relatively
again after the forty cold days of the
world night December 16 to January 25 stuck
in torpor's bed of self and loss of creation

Into which bed returns the one unageing
eternal thing she's rounded sweet beauty that yet
undoes and wakes and separates from all this worst
case torpor of self the one
best thing her own being like the world's large and with its color
warm and moist and coming green entry as the small
dark red plum buds still furled in
to themselves on long thin finger
branches start to swell out

The Divers

Beyond the stars
something else starts
out there in the time storms
where tonight
the steady radio pulses
emitted by the angel
are lost
There is no more firmament
only the divers
men
who locked into the love mode
with women
range and drift
in deep space
trying to pick up
those ghost signals
falling away
on negative parabolas
pulling the spindle out of true
then coming up for oxygen
and leaning back in
toward the One
Who Guides

Printed April 1987 in Santa Barbara &
Ann Arbor for the Black Sparrow Press by
Graham Mackintosh & Edwards Brothers Inc.
Design by Barbara Martin. This edition is
published in paper wrappers; there are 250
cloth trade copies; 150 hardcover copies are
numbered & signed by the author; & 26
lettered copies have been handbound in boards
by Earle Gray, each with an original drawing
by Tom Clark.

Photo: Robert Turney

TOM CLARK was born in Chicago in 1941. He received a B.A. from the University of Michigan and an M.A. from Cambridge University, where he was a Fulbright scholar. He has received grants for writing from the Rockefeller and Guggenheim foundations and the National Endowment for the Arts. For ten years in the sixties and seventies he served as poetry editor of *The Paris Review*, of which he remains an advisory editor.

His books include many volumes of poetry, from *Air* (1969) and *Stones* (1970) to three volumes of selected poems from Black Sparrow, *When Things Get Tough on Easy Street* (1978), *Paradise Resisted* (1984), and *Disordered Ideas* (1987). He has written biographies of Damon Runyon, Jack Kerouac and Ted Berrigan. His most recent book is a novel, *The Exile of Céline* (Random House).

Tom Clark lives in Berkeley, California, with his wife and daughter.